# *No Easter Sunday For Queers*

*A play by Koleka Putuma*

MANYANO MEDIA

# WHAT THE CRITICS SAID

[The] subject matter is poignant, hard-hitting and relevant. Koleka cleverly combines an interesting language of scripture with a contemporary voice to tell the story, and in the text we also have a strong sense of the theatrical potential of the play.

– Imbewu Trust judges

What remains upon leaving the world of *No Easter Sunday for Queers* is the imagery. Putuma's writing sits in the emptiness of what cannot be retrieved. Kabwe leaves the audience with a choral cold-burning cough of drowning/choking/possible-grieving. Emptiness is met with possibility. Etched into the debris is what remains when queer people are killed and not grieved; when justice is not received.

– Nondumiso Msimanga

Although an obvious heaviness pervades at face value, perhaps in honour of the subject matter, it is the light touches and how those cohere that power the story forward in the imagination.

– Kwanele Sosibo

The nauseating clash of religious dogmatism and sexualities which contradict hetero-norms is not something new. If you look at the issue of sexuality more broadly and infuse it with an historical glance at the culture and persecution of so-called witches, it simmers and seethes there too. Young playwright Koleka Putuma mines these old realities to create something new, fresh, fearsome and extraordinary in *No Easter Sunday for Queers*.

– Robyn Sassen

NO EASTER SUNDAY FOR QUEERS

Published in Cape Town, South Africa by Manyano Media in 2021
Kolekaputuma.com

First Edition, first printing, March 2020, Junkets
Second edition, first printing, April 2021
Published by Manyano Media

ISBN: 978-0-620-93135-9

Cover artwork by With Love The Agency
Author Photograph by Jarryd Kleinhans
Typesetting by Quickfox Publishing

Book production management by With Love The Agency

The body text of this book is set in
Minion Pro 10.5 pt on 15.5pt

The first edition of this play was made possible by sponsorship
from the following:

The Imbewu Trust
Tracy Saunders
Martin Hatchuel

The author acknowledges their generous support

# ACKNOWLEDGEMENTS

Mwenya Kabwe
For your friendship, your mentorship and dreaming this
text with me;
Thank you for stretching the characters and story into
dimensions that could hold a story like this, thank you for the
tenderness you wove into the text.

To the National Arts Festival, Distell and the Market Theatre
for giving the first staging of this play a platform and support.

*No Easter Sunday for Queers*, the poem, was birthed at
*Queer in Africa? The Cape Town Question.*
Thank you Zethu Matebeni for creating a space that would
lead me to this story.

CASA award
For giving me the support to write the first iteration of this play.

# CONTENTS

# DIRECTOR'S NOTE

**By Mwenya Kabwe**

What do you get when Religion, Race and Sexuality go to battle under the exquisite pen of Koleka Putuma? You get *No Easter Sunday for Queers*. As the cast and crew blessed and tasked with the inaugural staging of the work, we were driven by doing it poetic justice. How does one make a poetic experience for an audience that directly engages the searing violence at the heart of the play, the restless ghosts of the protagonists and the love of two people with redacted lives? With scripture, Beyoncé, a glorious cross-dressed chorus and a fierce cast and crew!
To walk through the battle ground every day, to sit with it in rehearsal cannot be done without a joyful loving community that orients its sights to a future in which *No Easter Sunday for Queers* is a 'museum piece', a protest play of old, a story of a time long gone when Queer murders remained perpetually 'under investigation'. Until then, I am deeply humbled by the opportunity to fight alongside my fellow creatives for a world in which we will live without fear or favour.

**2017**

Developed under the CASA Award, (a collaboration between the Playwrights' Guild of Canada Women's Caucus and the African Women Playwrights' Network), under the mentorship of Canadian playwright, Diane Flacks and Johannesburg-based, Zambian theatremaker and scholar, Mwenya Kabwe

**2018**

Further developed as part of the Imbewu Trust SCrIBE Playwriting Award

**August, 2019**

Staged at The Market Theatre, Johannesburg

**August, 2019**

An excerpt of the play, directed by British-Nigerian theatremaker, Femi Elufowoju Jr, was staged at the Roundhouse in London as part of Global Black Voices

# CAST

[First staging at Market Theatre, Johannesburg 2019]

**Napo/Daughter**: MoMo Matsunyane
**Mimi**: Tshego Khutsoane
**Pastor Nkosi/Father**: Lunga Radebe
**Choir Leaders**: Khanyisile Ngwabe, Tumeka Matintela

**Choir**: Amukelani Mabaso, Asime Nyide,
Chaunees Bokaba, Kgomotso Moshia,
Kgothatso Makwala, Khanyisile Zwane,
Lesedi Nkosi, Melusi Molefe Moagi
Kai, Nicola Niehaus, Okuhle Ngxe
Philangezwi Nxumalo, Pretty-boy
Sekhonto Rethabile Headbush, Scout
Fynn, Siphesihle Fakude, Sydney Ndlovu,
Tebogo Malapane, Thuthukani Lombo
Tshepo Matlala

# PRODUCTON CREDITS

[First staging at Market Theatre, Johannesburg 2019]

Playwright **Koleka Putuma**
Directed by **Mwenya Kabwe**
Music director **Nhlanhla Mahlangu**
Projection and sound design **Nicola Pilkington**
Lighting design **Jade Bowers**
Costume and set design **Thando Lobese**
Stage manager **Campbell Meas**

# AWARDS

Winner of the CASA Award, 2017
Winner of the SCrIBE Playwriting Award, 2018
Winner of the Distell / National Arts Festival Playwriting
    Award, 2019
Best Independent production at the Naledi Theatre Awards, 2020

# CHARACTERS

Note: Performers should all be Black.
Performers should be skilled in physical theatre and singing (should the staging require it).

**Father/Pastor Nkosi** Black. Mid 50s.
**Daughter/Napo** Black, 20 years old. Raised Christian. Queer.
**Mimi** Black, 33. Woman from the church. Queer.
**Choir** The director may choose the aesthetic and size of the choir

# SETTING

The set requires a multi-purpose pulpit.

# NOTE ON THE SCRIPTURE REFERENCES

The director and cast may choose to use these as reference points to guide or texture the scene.

NO EASTER SUNDAY
FOR QUEERS

## Scene 1: JUDAS

[Refer to: Mathew 26: 47–48]

*Father, Daughter and Mimi onstage.*
*Mimi stands quietly, at a distance, almost as a shadow or ghost*
*(or both.)*

**Daughter**   (*In a newsreader's voice or neutral voice (or both).*)
March 2015. Two bodies were found. One of them, water-tortured to death and the other strangled to death.

**Father**   (*In a preachy voice or stern voice (or both).*)
Luke 23: 20.
Pilate, wanting to release Jesus, addressed them again, but they kept on calling out, saying, 'Crucify, crucify Him!' And he said to them the third time, 'Why, what evil has this man done? I have found in Him no guilt *demanding* death.'

**Daughter**   The incident took place at the Holy Fire Baptist Church.

**Father**   Luke 23: 48.
When all the people who had gathered to witness this sight saw what took place, they beat their breasts and went away.

**Daughter**   One congregant says he saw the woman dragged by her hair to the pulpit, her body mopping the altar with her blood, and her lover begging for mercy while lying in her perpetrators' vomit.

**Father**    A limping voice from the back screaming, 'Father, –

**Mimi**    (*Whispering ghostlike, or out of turn, or both.*)
Forgive them; for they do not know what they are
doing.

**Daughter**    Some congregants, as well as Pastor Nkosi – also
identified as the father of one of the victims – were
taken into custody.
The ~~hate crime~~,

(*Pause.*)

The crime is still under investigation.

## Scene 2: PAROUSIA

[Refer to: 2 Thessalonians 2:9]

*FATHER stands behind the pulpit.*

*DAUGHTER sits in the congregation area where Pastor Nkosi (FATHER) can see her.*

**Daughter**  March, 2018.

**Father**  Kumnandi uba lapha.

**Choir**  It's nice to be here.

**Father**  It's nice to be here.

**Choir**  Kumnandi uba lapha.

(*Pause.*)

**Father**  I am a free man.

(*Pause.*)

    In him we are all free. Easter reminds us –

*MIMI walks in and takes a seat at her usual spot, slightly in DAUGHTER's view.*

    Easter reminds us that we are blameless both in the eyes of God and the law. On this sacred weekend She

**Daughter**  – He

**Father**     – He was crucified.

**Daughter**  He confuses the stories. He has memorised the one story very well and he is not able to forget the other one. Every Easter since it happened, he tells the one that pardons him, the one that makes him blameless in the eyes of God –

**Mimi**       And the law.

**Daughter**  And the law.

**Father**     As a symbol of his unconditional love, Christ bore the cross, even after Judas betrayed him, and Peter denied him, and the Pharisees tortured her –

**Daughter**  – Him.

**Father**     Even when the Pharisees tortured HIM.

(*Pause.*)

**Daughter**  He confuses the stories.

**Father**     Ask yourself, when Judgement Day comes, will you be Peter, or will you be Judas, or will you be the Pharisees, or the ones that rejected her?

**Daughter**  – HIM!!! HIM!!! JESUS FUCKING CHRIST, PAPA! GET IT RIGHT! *HIM*.

(*Pause.*)

**Father**    Him. The ones who rejected *HIM*.

(*Pause.*)

HE died for our sins. HE died to cleanse us of all unrighteousness. HE died because he was the chosen sacrifice. HE died so we could all be free.

Each year, in each sermon, I –

**Mimi**    – We.

**Daughter**  We die differently.

**Mimi**    Are murdered differently.

## Scene 3: THE BLEEDING WOMAN
## (or woman with an issue of blood)

[Refer to: Mark 5:25-29]

*DAUGHTER is standing at the altar; FATHER is standing in the centre, like someone who is about to officiate at a wedding. MIMI walks down the aisle carrying Bibles in various sizes. She stands across from DAUGHTER. The CHOIR sings 'What can wash away my sin?'. FATHER, MIMI and DAUGHTER look at one another, as if to signal the start of the ceremony. DAUGHTER reaches for MIMI's hands, MIMI drops the Bibles to reciprocate the gesture, and the Bibles fall to the ground. FATHER shoots MIMI a disgusted look, then reaches down to pick them up. DAUGHTER and MIMI stand on FATHER, whose face is now buried in the pile of Bibles. FATHER attempts to get up, but struggles with the weight of the lovers on his back. The hymn morphs into a disjointed melody of multiple wedding hymns.*

*MIMI in an officiator's voice, or preacher's voice (or both).*

**Mimi**      Who gives this woman to be married?

**Father**    (*In a restricted or pained voice, or both.*) I do.

*The CHOIR erupts in ululations, circling FATHER, MIMI and DAUGHTER. Father is lifted from the ground. At first the circle is joyous and celebratory. The ululation infused with wedding songs, gradually takes the shape of a swarm of bees attacking a thing they do not understand. FATHER is now pinned to the pulpit, like Christ or someone held hostage (or both). He is standing on the pile of Bibles pinned to the pulpit. A page from one of the Bibles is torn and stuffed into his mouth. DAUGHTER and MIMI move closer to each other; FATHER can be heard cursing softly in tongues; DAUGHTER and MIMI move closer and closer to each other; the cursing gets louder as FATHER walks towards them, occasionally stumbling. They get lost in the CHOIR, circling and singing. MIMI and DAUGHTER disappear behind the pulpit. FATHER knocks on the pulpit. MIMI and DAUGHTER emerge.*

**Father**   I've been looking for you!
Who do you think is going to lead the choir if you are standing here?

**Daughter**   Sorry, Papa.

**Father**   Sister Mimi.

**Mimi**   Pastor Nkosi.

*MIMI leaves.*

**Father**   What did I say about that woman?

**Daughter**   She was in the bathroom when I got there, Papa.

**Father**   Every Sunday?

**Daughter**   It won't happen again, Papa. I'm sorry.

**Father**   I don't want to see you with her, around her, near her, talking to her; I don't want to hear that you are accidentally seeing her, you hear me!

**Daughter**   Yes.

**Father**   She is just not right for you.

*(Pause.)*

For your relationship with God.

**Daughter**  Because?

**Father**  Are you questioning my authority?

**Daughter**  No. I would never, Papa. I'm just trying to understand.

**Father**  There is nothing to understand, only my instructions to follow.

**Daughter**  I –

**Father**  End of discussion.

## Scene 4: BINDING OF ISAAC

[Refer to: Genesis 22: 9-10]

*A little girl (*DAUGHTER*) holding a* sjambok, *her back to the audience, conducts the church* CHOIR *in a traditional funeral hymn. The* FATHER *looks at her, proud. As the hymn continues, getting louder and louder, the conducting becomes more and more aggressive.* FATHER *sings too; his voice can be heard above the other voices.*

DAUGHTER *now flings the* sjambok *about, as if it were a machete cutting through bamboo.*

*Bible in hand,* FATHER *approaches the* DAUGHTER.
FATHER *stands close enough for the* DAUGHTER *to hit his body. The action morphs from a standoff between the* FATHER *and the* DAUGHTER *into a friendly skipping-rope encounter.*

*The* sjambok *now goes from left to right, to a circular movement around the* FATHER's *body.*
*The* FATHER *jumps, still with Bible in hand. They are laughing, enjoying the game.*
FATHER *makes a mistake.*

**Daughter**  Out! My turn!

FATHER *now swings the* sjambok *around the* DAUGHTER, *gently at first, then faster and faster.* DAUGHTER *tries her best to keep up, jumping up and down. The* sjambok, *no longer a skipping rope, takes the shape of a weapon.* DAUGHTER *attempts to duck the* sjambok.

**Daughter**    Slower, Papa.
Papa, slow down, please!
Papa!

*Transitions into a church space, or a different space (or both).*

**Father**    Proverbs 13:24.
And he who spares the rod hates their children.

**Daughter**    How I first learned that being harmed means
being loved.

## Scene 5: GOOD FRIDAY

[Refer to: Matthew 27:27-56]

*Father on the pulpit.*

*Slowly creeping in is the sound of the Choir singing Beyonce's 'See me up in the club with fifty-eleven girls / Posted in the back, diamond fangs in my grill'.*

*The following dialogue happens on the beat of Beyoncé's 'Partition'. Mimi and Daughter sit centre in front of Father.*

**Father**    1 Kings 14:24.
And there were also sodomites in the land cast out before the children of Israel.

**Choir**    Drop the bass, manne, the base get lower / radio say speed it up, I just go slower.

**Daughter**    High like treble / pumping on them mids.

**Father**    1 Kings 22:46.

**Choir**    And why ya think ya keep my name rollin' off your tongue?

**Daughter**    When you wanna smash, I'll just –

**Father**    Romans 1:26.

**Daughter**    Another one.

**Father**    I sneezed a chapter and the beat got sicker.

**Daughter**    Yoncé ya'll.

**Father**     1 Timothy 1:9-10.

**Mimi**     Like liquor.

*Mimi places her fingers in Daughter's hand, Mimi pulls Daughter up.*

**Father**     Today's Gospel concerns two miracles, one the healing of an illness and the other the overcoming of death.

*Mimi and Daughter begin to move around Father, dancing or moving, at first as if they are praising or worshipping. Then slowly the dance starts to resemble bodies that are moving as if they are in a club or at a party. Mimi leans over to kiss Daughter.*

**Daughter**     No! Not here.

**Mimi**     I don't get it.

**Daughter**     Safety.

**Mimi**     So, You okay with fucking me in the bathroom of a church but not okay with kissing me in a club?

**Daughter**     It's different at church.

**Mimi**     Really!? How?

**Father**     These two miracles are closely linked, for both illness and death have the same origin, the same cause, they are both the result of sin. Both entered the world as a result of the sin of Adam.

**Daughter**     It just is. There's no danger there.

**Mimi**     For you, because they don't see what you are.

**Daughter**   I have to deal with shit just as much as you do.

**Mimi**   They wouldn't hurt you like they would hurt me.

**Daughter**   My father would.

**Mimi**   Has he done anything to you?

**Daughter**   Nothing, physically.

**Mimi**   He would.

**Daughter**   Would what?

**Father**   As the apostle John –

**Mimi**   – Paul, you mean Paul. For God's sake, if you are going to preach, then at least know your fucking Bible, Nkosi.

**Father**   As the apostle Paul says in his letter to the Orthodox Christians in Rome, 'The wages of sin are death.'

**Daughter**   When are you going to tell me about that?

**Mimi**   About what?

**Daughter**   I know you know the truth about what happened to her.

**Mimi**   Who?

**Daughter**   Come on.

(*Beat.*)

  Ruth.

**Father**   Firstly, let us consider the healing of the woman with the issue of blood. We should note that this issue of blood was not that monthly issue of blood suffered by all women, but something else. It had lasted for twelve long years.

**Mimi**   I don't want to talk about that in here.

**Daughter**   Between you and my father, I don't know who has more skeletons.

(*Next two lines are spoken together.*)

**Mimi**   I am nothing like him.

**Father**   I am nothing like her.

**Father**   Sorry. I mean. We have all been created in his image and likeness. So God created man in his *own* image. Genesis 1, verse 27.

**Daughter**   The ghost of your dead 'ex' comes alive every time my father's name comes up.

**Mimi**   If it weren't for your father, there would be no ghost.

(*Next two lines are spoken together.*)

**Daughter**   It was an accident.

**Father**   It was God's will.

**Mimi**   God's will includes drowning a 17-year-old lesbian in your fucked-up satanic baptism ritual – and for what? –

**Father**    Ruth didn't survive that baptism because she was God's sacrifice, a sacrifice that would cleanse this church.

**Mimi**    Can you hear yourself! She wasn't an offering or object, she was a person. A person I loved. And you drowned her.

**Father**    And you stood there and watched – why didn't you do something? If you believed that it was not God's will? All of you!

(*To the CHOIR.*) Why didn't you do something!? Why didn't you say something!?

*The CHOIR (As if they have been caught in a lie, or as if they are on trial, or both.)*

**Choir Member 1**   I was in the spirit.

**Choir Member 2**   I was praying.

**Choir Member 3**   Which Sunday was this?

**Choir Member 4**   I was high.

**Choir Member 5**   On the spirit.

**Choir Member 6**   What baptism?

**Choir Member 1**   Which baptism?

**Mimi**        Ruth.

**Choir Member 2**   Who is Ruth?

**Choir Member 8**   As servants of Pastor Nkosi.

**Choir Member 9**   Of God.

**Choir Member 8**   As servants of God we should never interfere with God's will.

**Father**   Her disobedience condemned her to death.

**Choir Member 1**   She chose her cross.

**Mimi**   I dislocated my throat.

**Choir Member 2**   Her mother was watching.

**Choir Member 3**   I moved to the front to help her carry the cross.

**Choir Member 4**   Which Sunday was this?

**Father**   I wiped her face.

**Mimi**   You suffocated her.

**Choir Member 6**   I screamed hallelujah.

**Choir Member 7**   She falls for the second time.

**Choir Member 8**   *Jerusalem, Jerusalem, lift up your voice and sing.*

**Choir Member 1**   She falls for the third time.

**Choir Member 8**   *Hosanna to the highest –*

**Mimi**   Stripped of her clothes /
His hands on her neck.

**Choir**   Crucify him; Crucify him; Crucify him; Crucify him.

**Choir Member 8**  *Hosanna to the king.*

*The rest of the CHOIR join in the hymn.*

**Father**          She.

**Daughter**          He.

**Father**          He was nailed to the cross.

**Mimi**          Her body, limp and wet.

**Father**          Taken down from the cross.

**Mimi**          Taken out of the water.

**Daughter**          He confuses the stories.

**Mimi**          They all return from the spirit. She does not.

*The hymn gets louder until it comes to an abrupt stop.*

## Scene 6: RUTH

[Refer to: Ruth 1: 16-17]

**Mimi**    ~~Most~~ Some of us have no name or lives that others
can hold on to, only a past, or a moment in the
past that can be picked at and dissected until the
examiner finds what they are looking for.
The thing you hide with polite conversation when the
visitors come. We have learned how to hold it all:
Scripture /
The upbringing /
The coming out /
The folding in /
The lovers who disappear while we are not looking /
The ones who disappear while we are /
The baptisms /
that drown us into silence /
The baptisms disguised as cleansing /
The baptisms where the holy spirit trumps reason /
trumps justice /
The baptisms ~~we~~ they call divine intervention.

**Daughter**  The Old Testament is a cage /
church three times a week /
A family I cannot shame /
A sinking ship with Peters who believe they can walk
on water /
I do not know if such powers are given to those who
do not believe /
Or those who doubt /
Or those who hoard two lives in one body /

Bodies so heavy they could sink themselves /
With all these secrets they keep contained /
How ~~they~~ we I tell no one /
And ask no one to help me carry a cross that crosses
us me out. Here, I am a shadow /
A dream deferred /
Uncertain in this language I love in /
Am aroused in /
The word is a prison /
Is a cell without bars /
Is a prayer-mat that zips my mouth /
And wears out my knees /
I am always in this position:
Repenting for something.

## Scene 7: GETHSEMANE

[Refer to: Matthew 26:39]

*Mimi stands behind the pulpit. Daughter sits in the congregation area.*

**Mimi**      Kumnandi uba lapha.

**Daughter**  It's nice to be here.

**Mimi**      It's nice to be here.

**Daughter**  Kumnandi uba lapha.

**Mimi**      1 Kings 14:24.
              And there were also sodomites in the land cast out
              before the children of Israel.

**Daughter**  Mimi is on the altar /
              spread-eagled /
              dripping in anointing-oil /
              she is preaching about a Calvary where the stone is
              not rolled away, but rolled over our bodies /
              where ~~our~~ her hands and ankles are tied with
              shoelaces /
              our arms flailing in baptism water at the foot of the
              cross /
              where we are drowned to death and crucified with a
              lover who cannot pick a paradise.

**Mimi**      1 Kings 22:46.
              He banished from the land the rest of the male and
              female shrine prostitutes, who still continued their
              practices from the days of his father.

**Daughter**   I am being baptised today.

**Mimi**   In like manner, Sodom and Gomorrah and the cities around them, who indulged in sexual immorality and pursued strange flesh, are on display as an example of those who sustain the punishment of eternal fire.
Jude 1, verse 7.

**Daughter**   I just want to get it over with /
to please my father /
someone is praying /
I drift /
wondering if the Holy Ghost is picky about the bodies it comes upon I wonder if the Holy Ghost will come upon me /
considering I'm not his type /
I wonder about the Holy Ghost's sexuality /
I wonder why the Holy Ghost comes upon people without their consent /
I wonder if the church uses the Holy Ghost as an excuse to do whatever the fuck they want.

(*Pause.*)

**Mimi**   Hello.

**Daughter**   Hello.

**Mimi**   Where's your mind?

**Daughter**   Here … with you.

**Mimi**   No escaping.

**Daughter**   How can I?

**Mimi**      The day you graduate, I'll take eleven cows to your father.

**Daughter**  One, I didn't know you endorse that whole cow-project. Two, why eleven?

**Mimi**      One, I'm fascinated with what a lesbian *lobola* might look like. Two, I don't know. I just want to rock up at the church one Easter Sunday wearing a crop top and booty shorts, and a truck loaded with eleven cows.

**Daughter**  And WTF are you going to say to him when you get there?

**Mimi**      *Lobola* for my pussy!

**Daughter**  He will love that, I'm sure.

**Mimi**      I'll tell him … I love you.

**Daughter**  …

**Mimi**      I love you, Napo.

## Scene 8: BAPTISM OF JOHN

[Refer to: Acts 11: 16]

*CHOIR Hymn: 'What can wash away my sin?'*

*Water is poured inside the pulpit. A flashback to the DAUGHTER's childhood. FATHER and DAUGHTER are playing with water, splashing each other. The DAUGHTER is trying to duck from the splashes, they are both splashing and chasing each other. FATHER catches the DAUGHTER and playfully dunks her in the water. She tries to escape his grip, as he repeatedly dunks her in the water.*

*The playfulness starts to resemble a baptism; the DAUGHTER is no longer enjoying the water and looks as if she is trying to signal for help. The FATHER now looks as if he is praying for the DAUGHTER and trying to restrain her at the same time. DAUGHTER slowly stops resisting, until she is staring blankly at FATHER and allowing him to dunk her repeatedly in the water.*

**Daughter**  Forgive me, Papa. I have sinned:
I love her.

(*Dunk.*)

**Father**  Out, Devil.

**Daughter**  Forgive me, Papa. I have sinned:
I love her.

(*Dunk.*)

**Father**  Out, spirit of darkness.

(*Dunk.*)

Daughter    Forgive me, Papa. (*Dunk.*) I have sinned:
             I (*Dunk.*) love (*Dunk.*) her.

(*Dunk.*)
             I love her.

*The CHOIR's hymn gets louder and more aggressive. The CHOIR, FATHER, DAUGHTER and MIMI collectively look as if they have entered another realm. The scene shifts from a baptism or drowning (or **both**) into something that looks like bodies slain in the spirit or bodies that have transitioned into a space of limbo (or **both**). After a moment, DAUGHTER and MIMI transition out of the spirit. It should be clear that DAUGHTER and MIMI are now inhabiting a different realm, a quieter and less chaotic space. The CHOIR's hymn (now gentler) is accompanied by FATHER preaching in what sounds like wailing and the sounds of someone who wants to vomit. This preaching does not and should not involve text: it is a preaching made of sounds. The sounds should language pain or disgust (or **both**). The FATHER's preaching and the CHOIR's hymn now serve as a bubble outside of DAUGHTER and MIMI. The bubble starts slowly to drift further away from where DAUGHTER and MIMI are standing, until the two are alone.*

# EPILOGUE: EASTER SUNDAY

[Refer to: Matthew 28:5-7]

*Preaching and a hymn can be heard in the distance. It slowly fades, until it is quiet.*

**Mimi**     Hello.

**Napo (Daughter)** Hi.

*The end*

KOLEKA PUTUMA is an award-winning poet, playwright and theatre director.

Her theatre works include *UHM* (2014), *Woza Sarafina* (2016), and *Mbuzeni* (2017/8). Her theatre for young audiences include *Ekhaya* (2–7 year olds), and *SCOOP: Kitchen play for carers and babes*, the first South African theatre work for audiences aged 0–12 months old.

Putuma was appointed as creative director for the 2019 Design Indaba Conference. She was recently shortlisted as one of four finalists for the Rolex Mentor and Protégé Arts Initiative for theatre. She is a *Forbes Africa* Under 30 Honoree, recipient of the Imbewu Trust Scribe Playwriting Award, Mbokodo Rising Light award, CASA playwriting award and the 2019 Distell Playwriting Award for her play *No Easter Sunday for Queers*, published by Junkets in February 2020, and played to sold out audiences at the Market Theatre in 2019.

Koleka Putuma is the Founder and Director of Manyano Media, a multidisciplinary creative company that produces and champions the work and stories of black queer artists and queer life.

**MANYANO MEDIA**

Manyano Media is a multidisciplinary creative company that produces and champions the work and stories of black women, black queer artists and queer life.

OTHER PUBLICATIONS:

*Hullo, Bu-Bye, Koko, Come In*, Manyano Media (2021)
*Collective Amnesia*, Manyano Media (2020)
*Collective Amnesia* [The Audio Experience] (2020)
Available from online audiobook retailers & streaming services

TRANSLATIONS OF COLLECTIVE AMNESIA:

Danish, *Kollecktivt Hukommelsestab*, Pub. Rebel With
A Cause (2019)
Spanish, *Amnesia Colectiva*, Pub. Flores Raras (2019)
German, *Kollektive Amnesie*, Pub. Wunderhorn Verlag (2019)
Swedish, *Kollektiv Minnesf.rlust*, Pub. Ramus. (2020)
Dutch, *Collectief – Geheugenverlies*, Pub. Po.ziecentrum (2020)

FORTHCOMING TRANSLATIONS:

French, Pub. éditions LansKine (2021)
Italian, Pub. Arcipelago Itaca (2021)
Portuguese, Pub. Editora Trinta Zero Nove (2021)

OTHER PUBLISHED PLAYS BY THE AUTHOR:

*Mbuzeni*, Contemporary Plays by African Women,
Methuen Drama (2019)

Publications and more available from kolekaputuma.com